Hemingway & Lorca
Blood, Sand, and Duende

Barbara J. Scott

DEDICATION

This book is dedicated to my beloved husband Michael who has given me his support in everything I've ever attempted.

CONTENTS

ABSTRACT

This study explores the cultural and historical influence of Andalusia on the poetry of Federico García Lorca and the prose of Ernest Hemingway, particularly the effects of the region's culture of life and death in their writing. This aspect of Spanish tradition found its greatest voice in bullfighting *(toreo)*, pure gypsy *flamenco* song, and the creative concept of *duende*. Even though Lorca and Hemingway were born worlds apart, their works are steeped in a civilization thousands of years old that was molded and shaped by numerous people groups, including the Phoenicians, Carthaginians, Greeks, Iberians, Romans, Vandals, Visigoths, Moors, Berber Muslims, and European Catholics. By examining the creative works of these men immersed in the rich heritage of Andalusia as expressed during the early twentieth century, readers can more fully appreciate Hemingway's novel *The Sun Also Rises* and Lorca's poem *Lament for Ignacio Sánchez Mejías*. They are masterpieces created by two great authors who influenced and changed the writing styles of those who followed them.

1 ANDALUSIAN INFLUENCE

Ernest Hemingway's *The Sun Also Rises* and Federico García Lorca's *Lament for Ignacio Sánchez Mejías* are masterpieces—one of prose, the other of poetry—created by two groundbreaking authors who influenced and changed the writing styles of the twentieth century. These two men were born worlds apart, yet in their works they both celebrate Andalusian culture, particularly bullfighting *(toreo),* pure gypsy *flamenco* song, and the creative concept of *duende.*

The purpose of this book is to compare the cultural and historical influence of Andalusia on the poetry of Federico García Lorca and the prose of Ernest Hemingway.

Hemingway and Lorca, who were nearly the same age, fell in love with Andalusia's vibrant culture and its unspoiled Alpine forests and rich farmland nourished by the Guadalquivir River—a place of gypsies and flamenco music.

Even though they were well-known in their respective literary circles, they were unknown to one another during the 1920s. Hemingway's work had not yet been translated into Spanish so that Lorca could read it, and Lorca's poetry had not yet been translated into English.

Instead, these men were like two brilliant planets in twin but opposite orbits, as they circled the same sun of Andalusia. Although unknown to one another, Hemingway and Lorca were nonetheless brothers joined together by the blood and the glory of Andalusian culture. However, there is some evidence that Hemingway, who became fluent in Spanish, discovered Lorca's writing during or just after the Spanish Civil War.

What makes the Andalusian culture so rich in creative energy? It has a unique pagan, Moorish, and Christian background. Andalusia's long history embraced numerous people groups, including the Phoenicians, Carthaginians, Greeks, Iberians, and Romans.

The Roman emperors Trajan and Hadrian were born in the region of Andalusia, and this southern Spanish setting also gave birth to writers like Seneca. Then in 711 CE the Muslims, or Moors as they were called, invaded from Tangier (now in Morocco) and drove out the Vandals and Visigoths who occupied the Iberian Peninsula.

In the eleventh century Christian armies campaigned to reclaim Andalusia, and the Arab Muslim state split into individual kingdoms that were constantly at war with one another. At the same time that Christians were moving south, a new invasion of Berber Almoravids (Muslims from North Africa) established rule from 1086 to 1147. They were then succeeded by another invading Muslim group known as the Almohads who held the reins of power in Andalusia after that date.

By the mid-thirteenth century, Ferdinand III of Castile recaptured most of Andalusia, except for Granada, which the Muslims held until their capitulation to the Christian armies of Ferdinand and Isabella in 1492. Muslim rule ended, and Spain has been a Catholic nation ever since. But rather than eradicate its early heritage, Andalusia embraced and incorporated the mysteries and beliefs of its diverse ancestry.

Background

Primarily, scholars have pursued two separate literary inquiries: one on the life and writings of Andalusian Lorca and the other on the American author Hemingway. Much like a genealogical chart, however, by exploring the history and influence of Andalusia, we can see how each writer is a branch, stemming from this rich cultural heritage.

There are no books that explore the similarities between the two authors, so in my study it has been necessary to scour the many resources available on each writer to find mention of the other. In September 2008, an article in *The Hemingway Review* written by Kristine A. Wilson titled "Black Sounds: Hemingway and Duende" used Lorca's concept of duende in examining Hemingway's *The Sun Also Rises* and *For Whom the Bell Tolls*.

As children, both Lorca and Hemingway were exposed to musical instruction by their mothers, as well as poetry. By a close examination of *The Sun Also Rises* and *Lament*, this book will show how an understanding of their musical heritage, both inherited and adopted, is necessary to fully comprehend the brevity and yet rich poetic and musical cadence of their work.

Another excellent resource that mentions how both Lorca and Hemingway were affected by Andalusian culture is Allen Josephs *White Wall of Spain: The Mysteries of Andalusian Culture*. In it, Josephs wrote:

> "As Lorca had written in his essay on *duende*, 'Spain is the only country in the world where death is the national spectacle, where death trumpets long blasts to announce the arrival of each spring . . . ' (1:1108). It was precisely for that reason that the young Ernest Hemingway would spend so much time in Spain seeking a purity of emotion in the atavistic

spectacle of death in the afternoon, a purity he could find nowhere else." (153)

Both men were deeply affected by the religion of Spain, and even though Hemingway had been raised as a Protestant, he converted to Catholicism after his exposure to the churches of Spain. Lorca was raised as a Catholic. The work of Hemingway and Lorca are filled with religious images, images of life and death, and of the passion of duende.

Theoretical Approach

In David H. Richter's book *The Critical Tradition: Classic Texts and Contemporary Trends*, Pierre Bourdieu is quoted as saying, "To understand the practices of writers and artists, and not least their products, entails understanding that they are the result of the meeting of two histories: the history of the positions they occupy and the history of their dispositions." (1320)

Therefore, the reason I have chosen this theoretical approach for my study of Lorca and Hemingway is that it allows me the freedom to delve into the cultural aspects of the Andalusian region, which affected them as authors and was of great influence in their writing.

New Historicism and Cultural Studies

The theory and term "New Historicism" was coined in 1982 by Stephen Greenblatt, a Renaissance scholar. In Richter's introduction to the essays on New Historicism and Cultural Studies he maintains that Greenblatt's definition was coined hastily and that ever since that time Greenblatt has endeavored to rename the theory as "cultural poetics" and to prove that what he does in a text is more a "literary version of cultural anthropology." (1320)

In other words, the theories of New Historicism and Cultural Studies suggest that a narrative—a story or poem—is a product of the greater narrative of social culture and history, and the author's personal life is just as much a narrative as the written text, bringing to bear upon the creative work every experience of a lifetime.

In her book *Critical Theory Today: A User-Friendly Guide*, Lois Tyson explains that:

> "For new historical critics . . . literary texts are cultural artifacts that can tell us something about the interplay of discourses, the web of social meanings, operating in the time and place in which the text was written. And they can do so because the literary text is itself part of the interplay of discourses, a thread in the dynamic web of social meaning. For new historicism, the literary text and the historical situation from which it emerged are equally important because text (the literary work) and context (the historical conditions that produced it) are mutually constitutive: they create each other. Like the dynamic interplay between individual identity and society, literary texts shape and are shaped by their historical contexts." (291-292)

Because Lorca and Hemingway were products of their personal histories and cultures, this book will analyze the culture and history of Andalusia, in particular its tradition of the bullring, as catalysts for the allusions used in the work of both authors. It is only when we understand this region of Spain that we can fully understand the music and poetry found in their writing.

By employing a close reading of *The Sun Also Rises* and *Lament for Ignacio Sánchez Mejías,* I will compare the similarities of Andalusian influence on Hemingway and Lorca, as well as the uncanny parallels in their separate lives.

Research Questions

The following questions guide this study of Andalusian influence on Lorca's *Lament for Ignacio Sánchez Mejías* and Hemingway's *The Sun Also Rises*:

1. How did the history and culture of the Andalusian bullring impact their writing?

2. What influence did the concept of duende have on the work of both men?

3. Why did the Andalusian culture of life and death affect these two writers so deeply, despite the fact they were born into privilege a world apart?

4. Both writers use constant references to the liturgy of the Catholic Church. How did a formerly Protestant Ernest Hemingway develop a relationship with the Spanish church as deeply as that of Federico García Lorca, who was reared in the Catholic tradition?

5. What impact did their early musical training have on the work of these authors?

6. Does Hemingway's prose show similar rhythms as the poetry of Lorca?

Delimitations

The delimitations of this thesis are intended to narrow the scope of enquiry and provide a more manageable examination of Lorca and Hemingway's work.

First, the examination is confined to the comparison of two major twentieth-century authors, both of whom worked and traveled throughout Spain during the 1920s.

Secondly, the discussion of Lorca and Hemingway is primarily limited to two works: *The Sun Also Rises* and *Lament for Ignacio Sánchez Mejías*.

Thirdly, this study confines itself to the cultural and historical affects of Andalusian Spain on their work. It does not pursue an in-depth study of the early period of Hemingway's life in Illinois and Michigan or his injury during World War I in Italy, the Spanish Civil War, or Lorca's trip to New York.

Finally, the study has been narrowed to examine the specific Andalusian influences of the bullfighting culture—the culture of life and death—that intermingled Catholic holy days with the festivities of the bullring; the musicality of these two authors' work; and the creative concept of duende.

Definitions

For purposes of this study, the following terms are defined:

1. **Duende**: A definition of the concept of duende is essential to the understanding of this thesis. Lorca writes in his article "The Duende: Theory and Divertissement" that duende "is a power and not a construct…." And later in his article when quoting Goethe says that duende is the "mysterious power that all may feel and no philosophy can explain." Duende is passion, but it is also "black sounds," Lorca writes, with "the roots that probe through the mire that we all know of, and do not understand, but which furnishes us with whatever is sustaining in art." Both Lorca and Hemingway struggled with duende in their work. It was the creative force that drove their writing, and they were both inspired by the duende of the bullring.

2. **Toreo**: bullfighting

3. **Flamenco**: For thousands of years flamenco has been the music—the song and dance—of outcasts, primarily the gypsy population of southern Spain.

4. **Gypsy**: According to the *Merriam-Webster Unabridged Dictionary*, gypsies are "one of a dark Caucasoid people coming originally from India and entering Europe in the 14th or 15th century that are now found chiefly in Turkey, Russia, Hungary, Spain, England, and the U.S., still maintain somewhat their itinerant life and tribal organization, and are noted as fortune-tellers, horse traders, metalworkers, and musicians." The etymology of the word gypsy is Egyptian, and Lorca believed Egypt was the original birthplace of gypsies, just as the Moors of southern Spain originated in North Africa.

5. **Afición**: Enthusiasm and a penchant for something. In Hemingway's *The Sun Also Rises*, the meaning is more related to a passion for bullfighting and is described in much the same way as duende.

6. **Thick description**: A term borrowed from anthropology by New Historicists, which, according to Lois Tyson in her book *Critical Theory Today*, "is not a search for facts but a search for meanings." Thick description focuses on the personal side of history, rather than highlighting traditional historical topics such as war or political change.

Summary

In this chapter, the foundation has been laid for this study of the cultural and historical influence of Andalusia on the work of Federico García Lorca and Ernest Hemingway. Primarily, the scope of this thesis has been narrowed to Spain in the early 1920s, and we will examine two critical texts: *The Sun Also Rises* and *Lament for Ignacio Sánchez Mejías*, both of which explore the uniquely Andalusian culture of life and death surrounding bullfighting, with its religious images and creative energy. The theoretical approach chosen for a close reading of these two works is New Historicism and Cultural Studies, which allows us a deeper understanding of the effects of a particular time and place on the work of these two authors.

In Chapter Two, we will examine past and current scholarship to lay out the need for this comparative study of Federico García Lorca and Ernest Hemingway.

2 REVIEW OF THE LITERATURE

In the first chapter of this study, I presented two interwoven theoretical bases from which to initiate an examination of the influence of Andalusia on the work of Federico García Lorca and Ernest Hemingway.

New Historicism and Cultural Studies examine the cultural, historical, and political effects on individual authors, their arts, and their texts, which are products of their life experiences. This approach gives us a framework to investigate how Lorca and Hemingway's work contributes to the thick description of 1920s Spain and how the history of that country, particularly the pagan, Moorish, and Christian influences of Andalusia, affected their literary works. The richness of their narratives can only be fully understood when seen through the lens of their individual identities and the fullness of their lives lived in that particular culture and in that particular period of history.

By reviewing the pertinent literature of these two authors and the region, this book will demonstrate how Lorca and Hemingway's work affected those around them and how they were changed by a particular place and culture.

Literature on Federico García Lorca

In Allen Josephs book titled *White Wall of Spain: The Mysteries of Andalusian Culture*, he traces the history of the Andalusian region in Spain, explaining that it is one of the oldest in Western civilization (3). Josephs is a university research professor and professor of Spanish in the Department of English and Foreign Languages at the University of West Florida, Pensacola. In his study of Andalusia, Josephs lays out for the reader the ancient origins and history of its culture.

He relates that thousands of years before the birth of Christ, the people who lived at the lower end of the Guadalquivir River traded with Israel during the golden time of King Solomon. Andalusia was known as Tarshish in the Old Testament, and in Greek writing it was called Tartessos.

Archeological evidence shows a primitive culture thrived on the banks of the river as far back as the megalithic era and was existent at the time of the Minoans. It was an ancient culture—a remote Mediterranean agricultural society—and in its pageantry of the bullring, it was a civilization that celebrated death. Its traditions and beliefs survived into the twentieth century, and its sensibilities were a natural part of the nation's psyche, unchanged through the time before the Spanish Civil War. (Josephs 3-4)

Lorca's concept of duende and his fascination with death was a result of the influence of this ancient Andalusian culture. Because Andalusia's roots are firmly planted in the region's earthy pursuits, death is a way of life, just as it is on farms around the world. Animals are born, and animals die. Crops are born from seed, and depending upon the weather, crops are harvested or they wilt under an unrelenting sun.

In ancient times, bulls were sacrificed to the gods, and when the Catholic Church held sway over the religion of the region, the dying image of the Christ was celebrated with the death of bulls in the ring; *corridas* are held every day during Holy Week. Josephs quotes Lorca as saying that "the innumerable rites of Holy Friday along with the most cultured fiesta of the bulls form the popular triumph of Spanish death." (Josephs 27)

The concept of duende is rooted, according to Josephs, in ancient Dionysian religion. Lorca called it the "spirit of the earth." Without duende—without the possibility of death—the poet believed there could be no life in his work. It is the struggle with duende, this Dionysian spirit, and the artist's ultimate victory over it that births creative work. (Josephs 95)

As Andalusia influenced numerous poets, writers, and artists, Josephs also maintains its duende is the essence of flamenco—the song of the gypsies. Lorca was fascinated with gypsy life, but he was not illuminating the modern gypsy society that steals and tricks, but rather a heroic gypsy culture, whose song and dance contained the rhythm of the whole Andalusian culture and its struggle with duende. (Josephs 153)

Andalusia's fascination with death is not a morbid concept, but rather it declares it is through acknowledging the final end of all things that one finds joy in life and gives life meaning. Life is a celebration expressly because of the struggle with death.

Federico García Lorca's *Selected Letters* are a window into the soul of the poet. In his own words, he paints his self-portrait, a more colorful one than could ever be achieved by his biographers. In the introduction to Lorca's letters, the editor and translator Dr. David Gershator writes:

> "Lorca had a personality that demanded and held attention through the force of its Andalusian color and charm. He easily dominated his circle with his musical talent and poetic high jinks. A member of his

generation, the poet Jorge Guillén, used to say to his companions on seeing Lorca approaching: 'Here comes Federico, now we can go on a spree of poetry.'" (Gershator v-vi)

For someone fascinated with the culture of death, Lorca was the embodiment of a life lived to its fullest. After translating the poet's personal letters, Gershator described Lorca as "supportive, sympathetic, generous, demanding, devout, whimsical, insecure, sensitive, and, since he was an Andalusian, punctilious regarding the formalities." (Gershator vii)

Gershator was one of Lorca's students in the late 1950s at Columbia University, and it was at that time, with the poet's permission and cooperation, that Gershator undertook the project of translating Lorca's personal correspondence. With the help of many people, including one of the poet's brothers, the work continued after Lorca's assassination by Granadan Falangists on August 19, 1936. (Gershator xiii)

In *The Demon and the Angel: Searching for the Source of Artistic Inspiration*, the author Edward Hirsch, president of the John Simon Guggenheim Memorial Foundation in New York, explores the concept of duende first articulated by Lorca. It is through the lens of the poet's duende—that struggle with the darkness, the spirit of the earth—that Hirsch examines the artistic temperaments and work of other world-renowned poets, authors, dancers, painters, and singers, as well as the work of Lorca.

As I will show in a later chapter, Lorca's sense of struggle with duende—the struggle of life and death—finds its full voice in the poem *Lament for Ignacio Sánchez Mejías*.

Another book that explores the life and personality of Lorca is the biography titled *Federico García Lorca: A Life* by Ian Gibson, who lectured in Spanish at the Queen's University, Belfast, and then became a Reader in Modern Spanish Literature at London University. In addition to Lorca's biography, he also wrote *The Assassination of Federico García Lorca*. He left academic life in 1975 and moved to Madrid to continue his work.

In the introduction to Lorca's biography, Gibson reveals the depth of his understanding of the Spanish poet. He writes:

> "My own feeling is that Lorca's best work, both the plays and the poetry, puts us in touch with our emotions and reminds us forcefully, in a world ever more computerized and machine-controlled, that we are an integral part of Nature—a Nature that all too often we tend to forget. 'Only mystery enables us to live, only mystery', the poet wrote beneath one of his enigmatic drawings. His work, due largely to the power of its earthy imagery, makes us experience that mystery more acutely than perhaps any other poet of the century." (Gibson xxii)

Christopher Maurer, one of the world's leading Lorca scholars and head of the Department of Spanish, French, Italian, and Portuguese at the University of Illinois in Chicago, offers an in-depth review of Lorca's work in his book titled *Federico García Lorca: Collected Poems*, the revised bilingual edition. He would agree with Gibson's assessment. In the introduction to his translation, Maurer writes of Lorca:

> "He seems to lead us urgently and directly to the central mysteries of human existence. In the thirteen plays and nine books of verse he was able to complete between 1917 and 1936—an amazingly short career—he spoke unforgettably of all that most interests us: the otherness of nature, the demons of personal identity and artistic creation, sex, childhood, and death." (Maurer xi)

Of course, one of the most illuminating pieces of literature on Lorca, *In Search of Duende,* was written by Lorca himself. In his explanation of duende, Lorca writes:

> "...there are neither maps nor exercises to help us find the duende. We only know that he burns the blood like a poultice of broken glass, that he exhausts, that he rejects all the sweet geometry we have learned, that he smashes styles, that he leans on human pain with no consolation..." (Lorca 51)

Literature on Ernest Hemingway

One of the most respected scholars on the life and work of Ernest Hemingway is Linda Wagner-Martin, Hanes Professor of English at the University of North Carolina, Chapel Hill. She has served as president of the Ernest Hemingway Foundation and Society and has published numerous books and essays on Hemingway's creative writing.

In her book titled *A Historical Guide to Ernest Hemingway,* Wagner-Martin sketches out a brief biography of the man, as well as includes essays from other well-known Hemingway scholars, who explore various themes in his writing.

For this thesis, I examined Hemingway's novel *The Sun Also Rises* and found Wagner-Martin's book *Ernest Hemingway's The Sun Also Rises: A Casebook* to be quite helpful in my study. Published in 1926, the novel was one of the first truly modern stories.

For those readers more attuned to the literature of Jane Austen, Charles Dickens, and other nineteenth-century novelists, Hemingway's style was jarring to their sensibilities. While Austen's characters developed leisurely through a long series of social interactions, Hemingway's style is cryptic. His characters follow no preconceived or logical action. They seem without purpose. (Wagner-

Martin 3) What does Jake Barnes want in *The Sun Also Rises*? What is his motivation? Hemingway's work is rife with subtext, which was not understood by most of the reading public when the book was first published. Scenes shift rapidly. His writing is full of action and his style terse, using an economy of words.

Edward F. Stanton's work *Hemingway and Spain: A Pursuit* is unique in Hemingway literature. Neither biography nor literary criticism, it is a personal journey that took eight years to complete. Stanton traveled through Spain to Hemingway's favorite haunts and followed in the writer's footsteps. He explains the hidden meanings—the subtexts—of Hemingway's prose, which lie under the surface of the novelist's work. Stanton's book contributes to the understanding of the ritual of the bullfights, the culture of Andalusian Spain, and the heroic model of the matador employed by Hemingway. Dr. Stanton is Professor of Spanish at the University of Kentucky and has written extensively on Federico García Lorca, Ernest Hemingway, and the Generation of '27.

Another excellent source of research is *The Cambridge Companion to Ernest Hemingway* edited by Dr. Scott Donaldson, Professor of English, Emeritus, at the College of William and Mary. It is an excellent source of scholarly analysis on Hemingway's major texts, includes a chronology of his life, and ends with Susan F. Beegel's essay on "The Critical Reputation of Ernest Hemingway." The bibliography is one of the most complete on Hemingway scholarship. For the purposes of this book, Allen Josephs' essay that explores "Hemingway's Spanish Sensibility" was most helpful in understanding how the culture of Andalusian Spain affected the writer and his writing.

Former Professor of History at Johns Hopkins University, Kenneth S. Lynn's biography *Hemingway* offers historical insight into the influences on the famous author from early childhood through his death by suicide. The chapters that explored Hemingway's life during the years 1923-1926 laid a foundation for the events that affected the author while he wrote *The Sun Also Rises*.

Hemingway explores the suicide of Hemingway's father, his own deep depressions, his obsession with bullfighting, his relationships with other famous authors of that time, his relationship with his wife Hadley, and his strong belief that the bullring was the perfect metaphor for life.

No review of the scholarship of Ernest Hemingway would be complete without mentioning Carlos Baker, a Professor of Literature at Princeton University from 1953 to 1977. He authored the biography *Ernest Hemingway: A Life Story* and edited the volume *Ernest Hemingway: Selected Letters 1917-1961*.

Baker died in 1987. The collection of letters opens a window into the soul of the man Hemingway as he corresponded with family, friends, authors, and his editor Maxwell Perkins. The letters are an invaluable source of research material about Hemingway's views of the culture of Spain and his travels there.

Summary

To compare the cultural and historical influence of Andalusia on the poetry of Federico García Lorca and the prose of Ernest Hemingway, it was necessary to begin my research with broad strokes. The Gale Virtual Reference Library provided basic historical knowledge of each author as well as bibliographic material for more in-depth study.

Project Muse, a scholarly journal database maintained by Johns Hopkins University, also was useful, as was the website maintained by The Hemingway Society, which is one of the most authoritative sources for scholarly information about Ernest Hemingway.

When using these search engines, key words used included the numerous permutations of the authors' names, their works, and other words such as: Iberia, Andalucia, Andalusia, Spain, bullfight, bullfighting, toreo, corrida, duende, matador, "black sounds," flamenco, Ronda, Granada, Malaga, Moors, and many others.

Since it was difficult to find the texts I needed through an online library, most of the numerous research books used in this study were purchased through online bookstores and used book dealers.

The only source I found that even approached tying together the work of Lorca and Hemingway was a journal article by Kristine A. Wilson titled "Black Sounds: Hemingway and Duende," published in *The Hemingway Review* in Spring 2008. It is for this reason that I undertook this more complete study to link how these two brilliant artists were affected by Andalusian Spain.

3 FEDERICO GARCÍA LORCA

Lorca's poetry was rooted deeply in the Andalusian soil, and it was in its cultural milieu that he wrestled with the duende to birth his poetic visions of life and death. He embraced the history of his homeland and incorporated it into his own soul.

"Lorca's image of Andalusia is, first and foremost, that of a historical melting pot, a fusion of diverse cultures: Oriental and Western, Greek and Roman, Arab and gypsy, Christian and Jewish," writes Christopher Maurer in the Introduction to *Federico García Lorca: Collected Poems*. "The poet considered *himself* a repository of these traditions..." (xix).

Lorca lived and breathed duende. He writes in the article titled "The Duende: Theory and Divertissement":

> "In the bullfight, the *Duende* achieves his most impressive advantage, for he must fight then with death who can destroy him, on one hand, and with geometry, with measure, the fundamental basis of the bullfight, on the other.

> "The Bull has his orbit, and the bullfighter has his,

and between orbit and orbit is the point of risk where
falls the vertex of the terrible byplay.

"It is possible to hold a Muse with a *muletta* and an
Angel with *banderillas,* and pass for a good bullfighter;
but for the *faena de capa,* with the bull still unscarred by
a wound, the help of the *Duende* is necessary at the
moment of the kill, to drive home the blow of artistic
truth.

"The bullfighter who moves the public to terror in
the plaza by his audacity does not *fight* the bull—that
would be ludicrous in such a case—but, within the
reach of each man, puts his life at stake; on the
contrary, the fighter bitten by the *Duende* gives a
lesson in Pythagorian music and induces all to forget
how he constantly hurls his heart against the horns"
(Lorca, *The Duende*).

Lorca's friend Ignacio Sánchez Mejías retired from the bullring in
1927, according to the notes in *Federico García Lorca: Collected Poems.*
Mejías loved poetry and pursued playwriting and even invited his
talented friends to help him celebrate the 300th anniversary of
Gongora's death.

But for someone who had experienced duende in the bullring, he
could not find fulfillment in his life outside the ring no matter how
varied and creative. He seems to have been inspired by the memory
of his brother-in-law Joselito to return to bullfighting.

"The only danger in bullfighting," Mejías told a journalist in 1934,
"is the danger of ceasing to exist. Joselito is alive. More alive than
Belmonte or I because he did die valiantly in the bull-ring, while we,
like cowards, are tucked away at home. We cease to exist, while his
presence is felt in every bullfight" (Maurer 943).

At five in the afternoon on August 11, 1934, Ignacio Sánchez Mejías is gored in the ring. Some sources say that Mejías was not gored at exactly five o'clock, but rather Lorca chose to use this specific time in his lament for his friend. According to Maurer (943) Mejías would die two days later of gangrene. Lorca laments for his friend in the poem that was written two months later in October of that same year.

It is interesting to note that Mejías's death turned Lorca's thoughts to his own future death, which would come sooner than he expected. Lorca is quoted as saying to a friend, "It is like my own death, an apprenticeship for my own death. I feel an astonishing sense of calm…There are moments when I see the dead Ignacio so vividly that I can imagine his body, destroyed, pulled apart by the worms and the brambles, and I find only a silence which is not nothingness, but mystery" (Auclair, 28-29).

When studying the poem in English, in the repetition of the line "At five in the afternoon" (1) the reader can almost hear the tolling of cathedral bells, marking the exact time when "death laid its eggs in the wound" (29). What we miss in not reading the section titled "The Goring and the Death" in Spanish is that Lorca used a combination of hendecasyllabic (eleven-syllable) and octosyllablic (eight-syllable) meter (Maurer 943).

What is the importance of the meter he chose? Hendecasyllabic verse was attributed to ancient Greek works and "used frequently by the Roman poet Catullus." It later became the standard for sonnets and epic poetry written in Italy, but was also employed by Spanish poets (Baldick 110-111).

Lorca maintained that octosyllabic poetry was a much older form, and yet I found in English that this verse form is found in "iambic or trochaic tetrameters" and used by numerous English and American poets, sometimes in a memorial poem (Baldick 176-177). Perhaps it stems, however, from an older form known to Lorca.

Lament for Ignacio Sánchez Mejías reflects the style of a mature poet, who laments the passing of his friend gored in the bullring. A lament is more visceral than an elegy. It is an intense mourning for the death of someone who was loved.

The first section titled "The Goring and the Death" begins after the main action. Lorca does not describe the fight with the bull, but rather the poem begins as Mejías is treated for his wounds: "At five in the afternoon. / It was exactly five in the afternoon" (1-2). This line will repeat every other line throughout the first section.

Five o'clock is important to Lorca. It fixes his memories in a specific time and place. The technique of repetition reminds me of some Psalms, such as Psalm 136, in which the narrator remembers the great deeds of God throughout time and ends his memory with the line, "His love endures forever." When the Psalm is read in a service, the congregation usually chimes in with that line.

Therefore, I assert that Lorca has set up this first section much like a liturgical event. Through his use of hendecasyllabic and octosyllablic meter, Lorca defines the rhythm of chanting voices in a Mass, repeating the phrase, "At five in the afternoon."

Both Lorca and Hemingway viewed the bullfight as a spiritual and liturgical experience. Perhaps five o'clock in the afternoon recalls the time of Vespers, the sixth canonical hour of the Church, whose service is traditionally held during late afternoon or early evening.

The "Vespers Walk" kicked off the Fiesta of San Fermin as described in Hemingway's *The Sun Also Rises*. Before the seven days of the fiesta—the seven days filled with action and blood spilled in the bullring—city officials and the people of the town made a solemn procession to the Church of San Lorenzo. It was a time of life and death, and it was only fitting to seek God's blessing on the men who might die in the ring. (Stoneback 242)

Or perhaps five o'clock is an allusion to a life cut short before its time. According to H.R. Stonebeck, in Christianity, seven is the most frequently employed symbolic number. It is a symbol of the universe, as well as the "seven days of Creation, the seven seas, the seven sacraments, the seven cardinal virtues, the seven deadly sins . . . " (Stonebeck 243) Lorca uses the number five to refer to the time of Mejías goring. The bullfighter would never complete the full cycle of life—the cycle of seven.

When I examined why Lorca broke his stanzas where he did, at first it was difficult to discern a pattern, until I saw that he is recalling the moment in a plot progression. If this poem were filmed, it might start with the camera on the boy, running across the deserted, blood-stained bullring, carrying the linen cloth. A linen cloth is normally used to wrap a dead body. The scene is silent except for the soft footfalls in the sand.

Now the camera draws closer to Mejías lying in the sand, but all we hear is the silence and all we see is evidence of the soft wind blowing flimsy gauze across the ring. The scene is focused on the wound and the futility of the ministrations to Lorca's friend: "and the bullring was drenched in iodine / at five in the afternoon, / death laid its eggs in the wound" (27-29). The third stanza focuses on the bullfighter as he is wheeled out of the ring, and in the fourth stanza, the reader suffers the agony of Mejías's pain when Lorca writes, "The wounds burned like suns" (45).

As in much of Lorca's other poetry, music and rhythm play a huge role in setting the mood and tone of the poem: "the drums of a dirge" (17); "the bells of arsenic and smoke" (19), and "Bones and flutes play in his ear" (35). It is the music of pain and suffering.

Lorca reveals to his readers the medical methods used on his friend by the words he chooses, and yet the moment is elevated beyond an emergency-room event. The wind scatters "bits of gauze" (9) as something is poured in the wound—probably an arsenic compound that oxidizes as it is set on fire to cauterize the wound and stop the bleeding. In America's history, gunpowder often was poured in a wound and lighted. The pain must have been agonizing. Iodine was the antiseptic of choice, but because of the unclean conditions, Mejías was doomed; gangrene was inevitable.

Lorca's use of simile and metaphor is seamless. The reader is so caught up in the story that at first it is easy to miss how he skillfully employs those poetic techniques to describe the scene: "The bed is a coffin on wheels" (33). This image clearly tells us the bullfighter is a dead man.

In the second section of the poem titled "The Spilled Blood," the reader echoes the poet's sentiment in the line, "I don't want to see it!" (53) Lorca paints a powerful image, when he writes, "Tell the moon to come, / for I don't want to see / Ignacio's blood on the sand" (54-56) and then exclaims, "I don't want to see it!" (57) Even the moon, the clouds, and the willows cannot hide the blood of his friend.

He remembers the burns, which conjures up the smell of burning flesh, for he cries, "Send word to the jasmines / to bring their tiny whiteness!" (64-65) Jasmines have a strong fragrance and would cover the stench of death, and their white blossoms would cover the ugliness of the wound.

One of the most powerful images focuses on the blood gushing in spurts from the wound. The poet writes:

> Don't ask me to see it!
>
> I don't want to feel the gush
>
> each time with less force,
>
> the gush that lights up
>
> the rows of seats and spills

over the corduroy and leather

of a thirsting crowd. (85-91)

They are simple words, yet so descriptive and moving. The "thirsting crowd" reminds the reader of the Romans crying out for blood in the Coliseum or the crowds who cried "Crucify him!" at the trial of Jesus.

Then Lorca switches to powerful similes to describe and honor his friend Ignacio. He writes, "His prodigious strength / was like a river of lions / and his stately reserve like a torso of marble" (106-109). The reader knows the exact meaning of Lorca's similes, although the images are fantastical.

In the next to the last stanza of this section, Lorca's lament reaches an emotional high pitch as he employs exlamatio—high emotion expressed in the form of an exclamation and apostrophe:

O white wall of Spain!

O black bull of sorrow!

O hard blood of Ignacio!

O nightingale of his veins! (134-137)

"No," he declares twice in the last stanza. "I refuse to see it!" (146) And yet the poet and the reader have seen the images quite clearly, and there is nothing that will wipe them from memory.

It is time to accept the tragedy and grieve, which leads the reader into the third section titled "The Laid-Out Body." Lorca writes, "Now Ignacio, this quiet man, is laid out on the stone. / It's all over…" (159-160). His first lines are brilliant metaphors, which employ stone and crying trees:

> Stone is a forehead where dreams groan
>
> For lack of curving waters and frozen cypresses.
>
> Stone is a shoulder for carrying away time
>
> With its trees made of tears and ribbons and planets.
> (147-150)

The rhythm of this section is more soft and flowing than the first two sections when the goring and pain and death are fresh. In those earlier sections, the end-stopped lines cause the reader to step in time to the dirge, and the emotion is high.

Now acceptance comes and Lorca uses a number of water images, such as "tears," "gray rains," "Rain falls into his mouth," "Love, soaked in tears of snow," "a river that has sweet mists and tall banks," and an exhortation to his dead friend to "Sleep, soar, rest: Even the sea dies!" (195)

The poem ends with the fourth section, "Absent Body." Lorca ends each stanza with the repeated words, "because you have died forever." There is acceptance in the breakdown of his friend's body; he is not remembered by the children, nor the bull, nor the horses, nor the ants. Autumn will return, but Ignacio:

> Like all the dead of the earth,
>
> like all the dead who have been forgotten
>
> on some heap of snuffed-out dogs.
>
> No one knows you. No. But I sing of you.
> (208-212)

Others will forget Mejías, but not Lorca, for he has composed a song that will not be forgotten. Once again, he introduces music, when he writes, "I sing of his elegance in words that moan / And I remember a sad breeze in the olive grove" (219-220).

This "Andalusian" was one of a kind, Lorca writes, "so open, so bold in adventure" (218). Because of this poetic masterpiece, Ignacio Sánchez Mejías will be remembered and never be forgotten. Nor will Federico García Lorca.

4 ERNEST HEMINGWAY

If Lorca was the son of Andalusia, Ernest Hemingway was the adopted son. Once the American embraced his new spiritual home, his writing reflected the culture of Spain.

In *The Sun Also Rises*, as well as most of his work after this time, Hemingway incorporates references to bullfights, sunny plazas, cold trout streams, Catholic churches, and the music of the fiestas, including flamenco.

It was in his struggle with the duende of Spain that the American gained fame for his portrayal of the country. He would always love Spain more than America. In a letter written to F. Scott Fitzgerald on July 1, 1925, from Burguete, Spain, Hemingway says:

> "To me heaven would be a big bull ring with me holding two barrera seats and a trout stream outside that no one else was allowed to fish....Then there would be a fine church like in Pamplona where I could go and be confessed on the way from one house to the other and I would get on my horse and ride out with my son to my bull ranch named

Hacienda Hadley and toss coins to all my illegitimate children that live [along] the road" (Baker 165-166).

Hemingway and Lorca, although unknown to one another, were nonetheless brothers joined together by the blood, sand, and duende of Andalusian culture. Hemingway, an aficionado of the bullring, actually attended at least one and perhaps more of Ignacio Sánchez Mejías's bullfights. In a letter to Henry Strater written from Valencia, Spain, on July 24, 1926, Hemingway says, "Everything is all shot to hell in every direction but in the meantime there are eight bull fights here starting tomorrow. Gallo, Belmonte, Sánchez Mejías, Nino de la Palma and Villalta, Miuras, Villamartas, Concha y Sierras, Murubes, Perez Tabernos, Guadalests and Pablo Romeros. Hadley and I are down here together. Pamplona was grand" (Baker 212).

Mejías was a good friend of Lorca, and Hemingway witnessed the matador's cape work in the ring. Although Lorca and Hemingway were both heavily influenced by Andalusian culture, as exhibited in the bullring, there is no evidence they ever met.

Even though Hemingway never used the word duende, he approached its meaning when he writes of the conversation between Jake Barnes and Montoya the hotel owner in *The Sun Also Rises*:

"Yes," I said. "He's a real aficionado."

"But he's not aficionado like you are."

Afficion means passion. An aficionado is one who is passionate about the bull-fights. All the good bull-fighters stayed at Montoya's hotel; that is, those with aficion stayed there. The commercial bull-fighters stayed once, perhaps, and then did not come back. The good ones came each year. (Hemingway, *TSAR*,136)

Then Hemingway writes in a later paragraph:

> Montoya could forgive anything of a bull-fighter who
> had aficion. He could forgive attacks of nerves, panic,
> bad unexplainable actions, all sorts of lapses. For one
> who had aficion he could forgive anything.
> (Hemingway, *TSAR*, 137)

Hemingway could only translate aficion as passion. Yet he explains that when aficionados of bullfighting first met Jake, and he was introduced as an aficionado, they would give him a type of "oral spiritual examination" to prove it.

In this "oral spiritual examination" Hemingway brought together the liturgy of the church and its religious symbolism with the duende of the bullring; both are filled with passion. The Passion of the church is the death and Resurrection of Jesus Christ on the cross. His was the ultimate struggle with duende, and Christ won eternal life. Hemingway describes the "oral spiritual examination" almost as if it were a sacrament of the church.

In chapter thirteen of *The Sun Also Rises*, Hemingway describes the interaction between Jake and the others testing his *aficion*. The native men of Spain believed that no American could possibly have that indescribable spiritual connection to the bullring. Hemingway writes:

> "When they saw that I had aficion, and there was
> no password, no set of questions that could bring it
> out, rather it was a sort of oral spiritual examination
> with the questions always a little on the defensive and
> never apparent, there was this same embarrassed
> putting the hand on the shoulder, or a 'Buen hombre.'
> But nearly always there was the actual touching. It
> seemed as though they wanted to touch you to make
> it certain." (TSAR 137)

In his book *Reading Hemingway's The Sun Also Rises: Glossary and*

Commentary, H. R. Stoneback makes the observation that the "rites and sacraments of the aficionado are marked with a specific linguistic and sacramental convergence with the rites of the Catholic church…" It was not only the words said, as if Jake were being baptized, but also the laying on of hands of a fellow initiate into the body of aficionados.

Stoneback goes on to explain that the rites of this passage in the novel "reminds the reader of what Hemingway had in mind when he discussed in a 1926 letter to Maxwell Perkins his projected book about bullfighting—'a matter of life and death'—and how it is 'the one thing that has, with the exception of the ritual of the church, come down to us intact from the old days'" (Stoneback 230; *Selected Letters* 237).

Lorca's religious images in *Lament for Ignacio Sánchez Mejías,* as I have pointed out in the previous chapter, are much in tune with Hemingway's descriptions of gorings in the bullring. His repetition of the line "at five o'clock in the afternoon" sounds like cathedral bells or a liturgical line repeated by the congregation during Mass. Both Hemingway and Lorca were deeply affected by the rites and sacraments of the Catholic Church.

In an article titled "Hemingway's Spanish Sensibility" by Allen Josephs, Salvador de Madariaga is quoted as saying about the novelist that "He was in Spain, inside Spain, living her life. And his two great works, *For Whom the Bell Tolls* and *The Sun Also Rises,* blossomed out of this implantation of the roots of that powerful American tree into Iberian soil" (Donaldson 221).

In classic Hemingway style, the author expressed his love of the country in much simpler terms: "Spain is the very best country of all. It's unspoiled and unbelievably tough and wonderful." (*Selected Letters* 107)

For both Lorca and Hemingway, the spectacle of the bullring was akin to a spiritual experience, and often the writers used Christological images to describe it. And they both viewed the *corrida* as liturgy.

Edward F. Stanton writes in his book *Hemingway and Spain: A Pursuit* about the religious imagery in *The Sun Also Rises*. He says, "The real structure of the book is to be found deep below its surface, in a profound, irrational undercurrent of primordial images and symbols embedded in the rhythmic, ecstatic prose" (Stanton 98). He goes on to point out that even "the great Andalusian poet and playwright García Lorca called the corrida a litury, an 'authentic religious drama in which a God is worshipped and sacrificed in the same way as in the Mass.'"

In addition to religious imagery, music fills the pages of *The Sun Also Rises*. Hemingway was obsessed with bullfighting and describes in detail (like the journalist he is) the fiesta surrounding a bullfight...the anticipation, the examination of the bulls and whether they are good ones (ones worthy of a matador with aficion), the drinking long into the night, the rhythm of dancers, the beating of drums, the whistling fifes, the blazing sun and burning sands of the bullring, the snorting bulls, the roar of the crowd, the goring of steers and horses by the enraged bulls, and the eventual blood sacrifice. The emotional struggle in every aspect of the festival, and especially in the *cante jondo*s—the deep song celebrated by Lorca—revealed the presence of duende.

In the novel Hemingway describes an older bullfighter, Belmonte, who has lost his duende. He now fakes his passion in the ring. Like Lorca's friend Ignacio Sánchez Mejías, Belmonte comes out of retirement to fight again. But he is no longer the bullfighter he once was; he is jeered by the crowd.

According to Kenneth S. Lynn in his biography titled *Hemingway*, it is no coincidence that Hemingway refers to Joselito and Belmonte in *The Sun Also Rises*. He knew well the world of bullfighters. In Paris, it was Gertrude Stein, Alice B. Toklas, and others in the expatriate community who first suggested Hemingway would enjoy the bullfights in Spain. So sometime in 1923, he and his wife Hadley traveled to Spain when she was five months pregnant. During his many trips to Spain, Hemingway learned the intricacies of bullfighting and picked up colloquial Spanish (Lynn 207, 209).

Hemingway's bouts of depression are well documented, but like Lorca, it is as if by struggling with death he found a life lived to its fullest. He had looked into the face of death during the war in Italy, and because of his experience, death lost its victory. As Lorca explained, there could be no creativity, no life, without the struggle with duende, and duende only comes when there is a possibility of death.

In 1918, in a letter written from Milan to his family, Hemingway talks about his injuries in the war and gives us insight into the end of his life when he committed suicide in 1961:

> "Dying is a very simple thing. I've looked at death and really I know. If I should have died it would have been very easy for me. Quite the easiest thing I ever did.… And how much better to die in all the happy period of un-disillusioned youth, to go out in a blaze of light, than to have your body worn out and old and illusions shattered." (*Selected Letters* 19)

In Spain he found that zest for life that stemmed from challenging death. He understood its culture of death lived out in the bullring, with all its pomp and ceremony. He found a spiritual home: Catholicism, where he found expiation of guilt in confession, and bullfighting, where he found the pageantry of the church played out on the battlefield of sand. The bullfights were a way for Hemingway to face death and cleanse the horrors of the battlefield from his mind. It was a way to face death without dying.

He expressed his love of bullfighting in a letter to his friend William D. Horne on July 8, 1923, in Paris:

> "You'd be crazy about a really good bullfight, Bill. It isn't just brutal like they always told us. It's a great tragedy – and the most beautiful thing I've ever seen and takes more guts and skill and guts again than anything possibly could. It's just like having a ringside seat at the war with nothing going to happen to you. I've seen 20 of them. Hash saw 5 at Pamplona and was wild about it" (*Selected Letters* 88).

Hemingway never pursued an interest halfway; he threw himself into learning everything he possibly could about the culture of bullfighting. He traveled to the bullrings of Seville, Ronda, Granada, Malaga, Toledo, Aranjuez, Madrid, and Pamplona to watch the bullfights. He interviewed bullfighters and ate and drank with them. Hemingway, like Jake in *The Sun Also Rises*, became an *aficion*.

On July 19, 1924, Hemingway wrote to Ezra Pound from Burguete, Spain, that the bullring offered immediate success, unlike a literary career:

> "Having been bitched financially and in a literary way by my friends I take great and unintellectual pleasure in the immediate triumphs of the bull ring with their reward in ovations, Alcoholism, being pointed out on the street, general respect and the other things Literary guys have to wait until they are 89 years old to get.

> "The Plaza is the only remaining place where valor and art can combine for success" (*Selected Letters* 119).

Or as he put it even more plainly in a letter to Howell Jenkins November 9, 1924, "Honest to Gawd Carper there never is anything like it anywhere in the world. Bull fighting is the best damn stuff in the world" (*Selected Letters* 131).

The Sun Also Rises, which brought Hemingway fame, was misunderstood by the critics of his time. To them it was a story of the superficial jazz age—the lost generation. In a letter written November 19, 1926 from Paris, to his editor Maxwell Perkins in New York, Hemingway gives future generations of readers a clear picture of why and how the book was written and for what purpose. The book's title was taken from a passage in Ecclesiastes. In the letter, he clarifies what he wants his audience to know:

> "Nobody knows about the generation that follows them and certainly has no right to judge. The quotation from Eccles.—one generation passeth and another generation cometh but the earth abideth forever—The sun also Ariseth. What I would like you to do in any further printings is to lop off the Vanity of vanities, saith the preacher, vanity of vanities; all is vanity—What profit hath a man of all his labour which he taketh under the sun?—delete all that. And start the quotation with and use only the 4th, 5th, 6th and 7th verses of Ecclesiastes. That is starting with One generation passeth away—and finishing with unto the place from whence the rivers come thither they return again.

> "That makes it much clearer. The point of the book to me was that the earth abideth forever— having a great deal of fondness and admiration for the earth and not a hell of a lot for my generation and caring little about Vanities. I only hesitated at the start to cut the writing of a better writer—but it seems necessary. I didn't mean the book to be a hollow or

bitter satire but a damn tragedy with the earth abiding for ever as the hero" (*Selected Letters* 229).

There is no doubt that at some point in his writing life, Hemingway came to admire, understand, and perhaps even be influenced by the work of Federico García Lorca. Unlike many casual readers, Hemingway understood that to read Lorca in his original language, one must understand the language of music. Both men had been taught to play the piano, and both had fine singing voices. In school Hemingway sang in the Glee Club and played cello in the school orchestra. (Lynn 24; Gibson 41) Some of Hemingway's first works were poems published in the magazine *Poetry* (Lynn 188).

In 1952 when Edmund Wilson was eager to learn Spanish, Hemingway recommended literature that might be useful to read, two books by Gerald Brenan—*The Literature of the Spanish People* and *The Spanish Labyrinth*. In the letter to Wilson, Hemingway refers to Lorca's work:

> "If you really want to learn the language you can skip a lot and start in with Quevedo. It is tough to cut your teeth on. But the fashionable thing of learning Lorca is completely stupid. His poetry is based on Andalusian music. If you do not know the disonnances [sic] of that music, or if you do not know Arabic, it is almost meaningless." (*Selected Letters* 794)

Because of his musical background, Lorca's work would not have been meaningless to Hemingway. He and Lorca had much in common, not only musically, but in their struggles to live life to its fullest in the midst of death. And they both viewed the *corrida* as liturgy.

Allen Josephs in an article titled "Hemingway's Spanish Sensibility" found in *The Cambridge Companion to Ernest Hemingway*, edited by Scott Donaldson, asserted that the early near-death experience in Italy "is directly related to his fascination with the primal scenes of tauromachy he was witnessing and recording in Spain" (Donaldson 229).

I believe it was more than that. In Spain Hemingway found his true home. He had first searched for that connection in Paris, but the sun-drenched landscape of Spain spoke to him at a deeper spiritual level. Its duende, as described by Lorca, took hold of Hemingway in that specific place.

Josephs writes:

> "By the time Hemingway wrote *The Sun Also Rises*, he understood deeply and intuitively the Spanish sense of toreo. And he used that sense, that hieratic or priestlike quality, to turn his undistinguished autobiographical draft of a few days at the fiesta of San Fermin in 1925 into one of the finest and most influential of modern novels, one that in the intervening years has only increased in fascination" (Donaldson 229).

Before Hemingway discovered Andalusia and its rich culture and heritage—its culture of life and death, its people of the earth, its song, its spiritual significance—he had only written journalistic pieces and short stories. In Paris he was learning to write; in Spain he learned to access those deep places of truth within himself that allowed the full expression of his art.

In Keneth Kinnamon's article "Hemingway, the *Corrida*, and Spain" found in *Ernest Hemingway's The Sun Also Rises: A Casebook*, edited by Linda Wagner-Martin, Kinnamon makes the observation that critics have underestimated the effects of Spain on Hemingway's psyche and work. Kinnamon writes, "An account of the effects of his contacts with the Spanish environment and character on his work should clarify the crucial result of his expatriation—that it has involved, to a remarkable degree, alienation from American and assimilation of Spanish values" (Wagner-Martin 126).

In Spain Hemingway bonded with a particular time and place and culture, and he produced one of his finest pieces of work because of it. The man and his writing came to maturity in the earth of Andalusian Spain.

5 BROTHERS UNDER THE SUN

While Ernest Hemingway and Federico García Lorca were born continents apart, they shared more commonalities than differences. It is well known that Lorca's sexual orientation caused him to desire other men, while Hemingway's persona exhibited his love of women and a virile lifestyle. Yet setting aside this aspect of their personalities, it is easy to see how both authors appreciated and craved the simplicity and primitive nature of an unspoiled land. They both found it in Andalusian Spain, with its ancient culture and history rooted in pagan, Moorish, and Christian beginnings.

Over the centuries Spain developed a culture of life and death; one could not exist without the struggle with the other. Both Lorca and Hemingway were preoccupied in their private lives and in their writings with the topic of death. Lorca often rehearsed his own death by having his friends take pictures of him in the death pose. (Gibson photo 7) He wrote that the goring and death of Meijas and his elegy to the bullfighter was an "apprenticeship" for his own death. Hemingway, after facing death in one of the first battles of World War I in Italy, also seemed obsessed with death in his writings, particularly in his portrayal of the spectacle in the bullring. This motif of death runs through all of their work. Both would end their lives violently; Lorca was executed during the Spanish Civil War, and Hemingway ended his life with suicide, just as his father had before him.

Both Lorca and Hemingway suffered from severe bouts of depression, followed by the obsessive need to live life to its fullest, challenging death in their lives and work. Lorca would define his creative struggles with the duende, which would only come when there was the possibility of death.

Hemingway experienced this same duende, although he did not use the same words. He would call it aficion or passion. After a bout of depression Hemingway would go on an extended spree of writing, drinking, and loving. I speculate that both authors suffered from a bipolar condition that took them from the depths of blackness to manic episodes of ecstatic or orgasmic activity in their work and lives.

The rhythm of music is another motif running through Lorca and Hemingway's writing. Both had studied music from an early age, learning to play the piano and sing, and it was an important part of their inner and outer lives. Even Hemingway said that a reader could not understand Lorca's work without a knowledge of Andalusian music, with its Moorish roots. Hemingway's prose style also exhibited a sparse, yet rhythmic musicality. Edward F. Stanton in his book *Hemingway and Spain* wrote:

> "Hemingway was very aware of the rhythmic or poetic quality of his prose, but he felt reluctant to discuss it in public; it would have been a profanation of an artistic secret to reveal it openly. 'It is only with alchemy that you combine poetry and prose,' he once said. It was not so much the words as the rhythm that 'makes the emotion.'" (Stanton 37)

According to Stanton, sometimes to achieve the poetic rhythm in his prose, Hemingway resorted to grammatical "errors." But the rhythm was more important than grammar, and he most often won battles with copyeditors who would seek to destroy that rhythm.

Lorca battled the same type of editors who would change his poetry in print to suit grammatical rules. In *Federico García Lorca: Selected Letters*, he laments to his friend Jorge Guillen in 1927 that when his ballads were printed in *Litoral,* they were filled with errors. He wrote:

> "They contained more than ten(!) enormous errata and were completely ruined. Most of all the ballad of Antoñito el Camborio. What great anguish it caused me, dear Jorge, to see them broken, undone, without that *strength* and flintlike *grace* that for me they seem to possess! Emilio [Prados] agreed to send me proofs but he never did. The morning when I received the magazine I cried, I literally *cried,* it was such a shame" (*Selected Letters* 94).

In *The Sun Also Rises,* as well as in *Lament for Ignacio Sánchez Mejías,* the authors employed Dionysian, Mithraic, and elegiac language when speaking of the liturgy of the bullring. Its spectacle mirrored the Mass of the Catholic Church in which the congregation celebrates the life, death, and Resurrection of Jesus Christ in the Sacrament of Communion—the drinking of wine and eating of bread, the blood and body of Christ.

Yet this blood sacrifice is even older than the Christian church. It begins with the blood sacrifice of bulls by Abraham to his God and is found in the Mithraic rites of the Iberians. Even the wine consumed during the fiesta in *The Sun Also Rises* is a symbol of the blood spilled in the ring and celebrated in the Church. In 1984 Stanton interviewed Antonio González, the owner and host of the restaurant Botin in Madrid once frequented by Hemingway. González told Stanton, "The wine in that novel is not there by accident. It is almost a sacrament; through wine Ernesto knew that the Dionysian man could emerge. That is what he was seeking in Spain from the very beginning" (Stanton 4).

Implications for further research

Abundant research has been done on the lives and work of both Federico García Lorca and Ernest Hemingway, but little on comparisons of these two great authors. Kristine A. Wilson chose to look at the concept of duende in the work of both artists in her article titled "Black Sounds: Hemingway and Duende," but the field is wide open to explore this relationship.

Certainly, Hemingway was affected by the same Andalusian cultural and historical milieu as Lorca, but even their childhoods, although spent on two different continents, show similarities.

Research could delve deeper into the musicality found in the works of both authors. Religious imagery is another topic to be explored in the future. Their struggles with depression and how it affected their work could be documented. The fascination with the culture of life and death could be explored in the works of both Lorca and Hemingway.

For the purposes of this study I have confined its parameters to examining only two works: the poem *Lament for Ignacio Sánchez Mejías* and *The Sun Also Rises*. Future researchers could explore the suggested themes, as well as many others, in Lorca and Hemingway's other work.

Other researchers could view these two men through the modernist lens and how the twentieth century left its stamp on them personally and in their work.

Since "little effort has been made to isolate and examine the Spanish influence on Hemingway," Kinnamon writes (Wagner-

Martin *Casebook* 126), an in-depth study of Hemingway's transformation as a writer of primarily Hispanic subjects could be compared and contrasted with Lorca's work as a native of Andalusian Spain.

In this section several avenues of research have been sketched out for future scholars from a cultural and historical theoretical approach, but other theoretical theories offer a treasure trove of research possibilities, including the use of feminist theory to investigate how Lorca and Hemingway portray women in their work. It is the hope of this author that this work will spark more in-depth research on these two giants of modern literature.

WORKS CITED

"Andalusia." Encyclopædia Britannica. 2008. Encyclopædia
   Britannica Online. 1 Mar. 2008
   <http://search.eb.com/eb/article-9007417>.

Auclair, Marcelle. Enfance et mort de García Lorca. Paris: Éditions
   du Seuil, 1968.

Baldick, Chris. Oxford Concise Dictionary of Literary Terms.
   Oxford: Oxford UP, 2004.

Baker, Carlos. Ernest Hemingway: A Life Story. New York: Charles
   Scribner's Sons, 1969.

---. Hemingway: The Writer as Artist. Princeton, NJ: Princeton UP,
   1952, 1980.

---. Ed. Hemingway and His Critics. New York: Hill and Wang, 1961.

Berg, A. Scott. Max Perkins: Editor of Genius. New York: E.P.
   Dutton, 1978.

Casanova-fernandez, Vanesa. "Spain and the Middle East."
   Encyclopedia of the Modern Middle East and North Africa.
   Vol. 4. 2nd ed. New York: Macmillan Reference USA, 2004.
   2083-2085. Gale Virtual Reference Library. Gale.
   NATIONAL UNIV. 14 Oct. 2008
   <http://go.galegroup.com/ps/start.do?p=GVRL&u=nu_ma
   in>.

De Ros, Xon. "Science and myth in Llanto por Ignacio Sánchez
   Mejías." Modern Language Review 95:1 (2000): 114-126.

Donaldson, Scott, ed. The Cambridge Companion to Ernest
   Hemingway. Cambridge: Cambridge UP, 1996.

"Ernest Hemingway." Authors and Artists for Young Adults. Vol.
19. Gale Research, 1996. Reproduced in Biography Resource
Center. Farmington Hills, Mich.: Gale, 2008.
http://galenet.galegroup.com/servlet/BioRC

"Ernest (Miller) Hemingway: 1899-1961." Contemporary Authors
Online, Gale, 2008. Reproduced in Biography Resource
Center. Farmington Hills, Mich.: Gale, 2008.
http://galenet.galegroup.com/servlet/BioRC

"Federico García Lorca." Authors and Artists for Young Adults,
Volume 46. Gale Group, 2002. Reproduced in Biography
Resource Center. Farmington Hills, Mich.: Gale, 2008.
http://galenet.galegroup.com/servlet/BioRC

"García Lorca, Federico (1898-1936)." Dictionary of Literary
Influences: The Twentieth Century, 1914-2000. Ed. John
Powell. Westport, CT: Greenwood Press, 2004. 188-190.
Gale Virtual Reference Library. Gale. NATIONAL UNIV.
14 Oct. 2008
<http://go.galegroup.com/ps/start.do?p=GVRL&u=nu_ma
in>.

Gervais, David. "The Spanish Civil War: Dreams and Nightmares."
Cambridge Quarterly 31:3 (2002): 272-276.

Gibson, Ian. Federico García Lorca: A Life. New York: Pantheon
Books, 1989.

---. The Assassination of Federico García Lorca. New York: Penguin
Books, 1983.

Hemingway, Ernest. The Sun Also Rises. New York: Scribner, 1926,
1954, 2006.

---. Ernest Hemingway: Selected Letters 1917-1961. Baker, Carlos, ed.
Scribner Classics Edition. New York: Scribner, 2003.

Hirsch, Edward. The Demon and the Angel: Searching for the Source of Artistic Inspiration. Orlando: Harcourt, 2002.

Josephs, Allen. White Wall of Spain: The Mysteries of Andalusian Culture. Pensacola: University of West Florida Press, 1990. Ames, IA: Iowa State UP, 1983.

---. "Toreo: The Moral Axis of The Sun Also Rises." The Hemingway Review 6:1 (1986): 88-99.

Lorca, Federico García. Collected Poems. Ed. Christopher Maurer. New York: Farrar, Straus and Giroux, 2002.

---. In Search of Duende. Ed. Christopher Mauer. New York: New Directions Publishing, 1955, 1998.

---. Federico García Lorca: Selected Letters. Ed. David Gershator. New York: New Directions Publishing, 1954, 1977, 1983.

---. "The Duende: Theory and Divertissement," Lorca, Federico García. 1930. 1 Mar. 2008 www.musicpsyche.org/Lorca-Duende.htm.

Lynn, Kenneth S. Hemingway. Cambridge: Harvard University Press, 1987.

Mandel, Miriam B. "A reader's guide to Pilar's bullfighters: Untold histories in For Whom the Bell Tolls." The Hemingway Review 15.1 (1995): 94-104.

McFarland, Ron. "Hemingway and the poets." The Hemingway Review 20.2 (2001): 37-58. Humanities Module. ProQuest. National University Library, San Diego, CA. 10 Sep. 2008 <http://www.proquest.com.ezproxy.nu.edu/>

Miller, Montserrat. "The Iberian Peninsula." Encyclopedia of

European Social History. Vol. 1: Methods & Theory/Periods/Regions, Nations, Peoples/Europe & the World. Detroit: Charles Scribner's Sons, 2001. 307-319. Gale Virtual Reference Library. Gale. NATIONAL UNIV. 14 Oct. 2008 <http://go.galegroup.com/ps/start.do?p=GVRL&u=nu_ma in>.\

Mooney, Carolyn J. "Removing the bull from the bullfight: A historian busts myths." The Chronicle of Higher Education 10 Sep. 1999: B2. Research Library Core. ProQuest. National University Library, San Diego, CA. 10 Sep. 2008 <http://www.proquest.com.ezproxy.nu.edu/>

Morris, C. Brian. Son of Andalusia: The Lyrical Landscapes of Federico García Lorca. Nashville: Vanderbilt UP, 1997.

Rae, Patricia, ed. Modernism and Mourning. Lewisburg: Bucknell UP, 2007.

Richter, David H., ed. The Critical Tradition: Classic Texts and Contemporary Trends, 3rd ed. Boston: Bedford/St. Martin's, 2007.

Rodríguez-Pazos, Gabriel. "Not So True, Not So Simple: The Spanish Translations of The Sun Also Rises." The Hemingway Review 23.2 (2004): 47-65,3. Humanities Module. ProQuest. National University Library, San Diego, CA. 10 Sep. 2008 <http://www.proquest.com.ezproxy.nu.edu/>

Simón, Francisco Marco. "Iberian Religion." Encyclopedia of Religion. Vol. 6. 2nd ed. Detroit: Macmillan Reference USA, 2005. 4249-4254. Gale Virtual Reference Library. Gale. NATIONAL UNIV. 14 Oct. 2008

<http://go.galegroup.com/ps/start.do?p=GVRL&u=nu_main >.

Stanton, Edward F. Hemingway and Spain. Seattle: University of
     Washington Press, 1989.

Stoneback, H.R. Reading Hemingway's *The Sun Also Rises*: Glossary
     and Commentary. Kent, OH: The Kent State UP, 2007.

Totton, Robin. Song of the Outcasts: An Introduction to Flamenco.
     Portland: Amadeus Press.

Trogdon, Robert W., ed. Ernest Hemingway: A Literary Reference.
     New York: Carroll & Graf Publishers, 1999, 2002.

Tyson, Lois. Critical Theory Today: A User-Friendly Guide, 2nd ed.
     New York: Routledge/Taylor & Francis Group, 2006.

Wagner-Martin, Linda, ed. A Historical Guide to Ernest Hemingway.
     New York, Oxford UP, 2000.

---. Hemingway: Seven Decades of Criticism. East Lansing: Michigan
     State UP, 1998.

---. Ernest Hemingway's *The Sun Also Rises*: A Casebook. New York:
     Oxford UP, 2002.

Wilson, Kristine A. "'BLACK SOUNDS': HEMINGWAY AND
     DUENDE." The Hemingway Review 27.2 (2008): 74-95,
     5. Humanities Module. ProQuest. National University
     Library, San Diego, CA. 10 Sep.
     2008 <http://www.proquest.com.ezproxy.nu.edu/>

ABOUT THE AUTHOR

Barbara J. Scott has more than thirty years of publishing experience, ranging from newspapers and magazines to books. As a senior acquisitions editor, she is credited for kicking off a well-rounded series of bestselling young adult novels at Zondervan and quality, highly reviewed novels at Abingdon Press. Barbara worked with both fiction and nonfiction authors and sold their work to numerous publishers while acting as a literary agent for WordServe Literary Group. She also is a published author, and her educational background includes a M.A. and a B.A. in English. Barbara lives in the Nashville area.

Made in the USA
Lexington, KY
06 September 2017